Anti-Slavery Poems

John Pierpont

LITERATURE HOUSE / GREGG PRESS

Upper Saddle River, N. J.

Republished in 1970 by

LITERATURE HOUSE

an imprint of The Gregg Press

121 Pleasant Avenue

Upper Saddle River, N. J. 07458

Standard Book Number—8398-1570-0

Library of Congress Card—71-104544

118957

Printed in United States of America

THE

ANTI-SLAVERY POEMS

OF

JOHN PIERPONT.

'Was it right,
While my unnumbered brethren toiled and bled,
That I should dream away the entrusted hours
On rose-leaf beds, pampering the coward heart,
With feelings all too delicate for use?' — COLERIDGE.

BOSTON:
PUBLISHED BY OLIVER JOHNSON,
And Sold at 25 Cornhill.
1843.

OLIVER JOHNSON, PRINTER,

47 Court Street.

TO THE READER.

Thɪs compilation embraces all the Poems that Mr. Pɪᴇʀᴘᴏɴᴛ has written on the subject of Slavery. Several of them are contained in the complete collection of his Poems, published in 1840.* Alluding to these, in his preface to that volume, the author says: — 'Though some of my friends may grieve, and wish that I had been more prudent than to write the pieces that touch thus upon Human Liberty, and upon the outrageous wrongs that, in these days and in this our land, it has suffered, their grandchildren will thank me, and *may* be freer men for them.' There are others of Mr. Pɪᴇʀᴘᴏɴᴛ's friends, who, feeling that they *are* freer men for them, will not leave it for their grandchildren to thank him. It was to gratify such, and to increase their number, till the American slave, too, shall be free, that the compiler obtained the author's permission to publish this selection for them to circulate; sharing their conviction, that the fit offering of gratitude to the pious man and the poet is the diffusion of his soul-stirring words and ennobling thoughts.

Bᴏsᴛᴏɴ, May 25, 1843.

* '*Airs of Palestine, and other Poems, by John Pierpont.*' Boston: *James Munroe and Co.*

CONTENTS.

———

ANTI-SLAVERY POEMS.

PRAYER OF THE CHRISTIAN.

WITH thy pure dews and rains,
Wash out, O God, the stains,
   From Afric's shore;
And, while her palm trees bud,
Let not her children's blood,
With her broad Niger's flood,
   Be mingled more!

Quench, righteous God, the thirst,
That Congo's sons hath cursed —
   The thirst for gold!

Shall not thy thunders speak,
Where Mammon's altars reek,
Where maids and matrons shriek,
    Bound, bleeding, sold?

Hear'st thou, O God, those chains,
Clanking on Freedom's plains,
    By Christians wrought?
Them, who those chains have worn,
Christians from home have torn,
Christians have hither borne,
    Christians have bought!

Cast down, great God, the fanes
That, to unhallowed gains,
    Round us have risen —
Temples, whose priesthood pore
Moses and Jesus o'er,
Then bolt the black man's door,
    The poor man's prison!

Wilt thou not, Lord, at last,
From thine own image, cast

Away all cords,
But that of love, which brings
Man, from his wanderings,
Back to the King of kings,
The Lord of lords!
1829.

A WORD FROM A PETITIONER.

———◆———

WHAT! our petitions spurned!   The prayer
　　Of thousands, — tens of thousands, — cast
Unheard, beneath your Speaker's chair!
　　But ye *will* hear us, first or last.
The thousands that, last year, ye scorned,
Are millions now.   Be warned!   Be warned!

Turn not, contemptuous, on your heel; —
　　It is not for an act of grace
That, suppliants, at your feet we kneel, —
　　We stand; — we look you in the face,
And say, — and we have weighed the word, —
That our petitions SHALL be heard.

There are two powers above the laws
    Ye make or mar : — they 're our allies.
Beneath their shield we 'll urge our cause,
    Though *all* your hands against us rise.
We 've proved them, and we know their might;
The CONSTITUTION and the RIGHT.

We say not, ye shall snap the links
    That bind you to your dreadful slaves;
Hug, if ye will, a corpse that stinks,
    And toil on with it to your graves!
But, that ye *may* go, coupled thus,
Ye never shall make slaves of *us.*

And what, but more than slaves, are they,
    Who 're told they ne'er shall be denied
The right of prayer; yet, when they pray,
    Their prayers, *unheard,* are thrown aside?
Such mockery *they* will tamely bear,
Who 're fit an iron chain to wear.

' The ox, that treadeth out the corn,
    Thou shalt not muzzle.' — Thus saith God.
And will ye muzzle the free-born, —

The *man*, — the owner of the sod, —
Who 'gives the grazing ox his meat,'
And you, — his servants here, — your seat?

There 's a cloud, blackening up the sky!
    East, west, and north its curtain spreads;
Lift to its muttering folds your eye!
    Beware! for, bursting on your heads,
It hath a force to bear you down; —
'T is an insulted people's frown.

Ye may have heard of the Soultán,
    And how his Janissaries fell!
Their barracks, near the Atmeidán,
    He barred, and fired; — and their death-yell
Went to the stars, — and their blood ran,
In brooks, across the Atmeidán.

The despot spake; and, in one night,
    The deed was done.   He wields, alone,
The sceptre of the Ottomite,
    And brooks no brother near his throne.
Even now, the bow-string, at his beck,
Goes round his mightiest subject's neck;

Yet will *he*, in his saddle, stoop, —
   I 've seen him, in his palace-yard, —
To take petitions from a troop
   Of *women*, who, behind his guard,
Come up, their several suits to press,
To state their wrongs, and ask redress.

And these, into his house of prayer,
   I 've seen him take ; and, as he spreads
His own before his Maker there,
   These women's prayers he hears or reads ; —
For, while he wears the diadem,
He is instead of God to them.

And this he *must* do. He may grant,
   Or may deny ; but *hear* he must.
Were his Seven Towers all adamant,
   They 'd soon be levelled with the dust,
And 'public feeling' make short work, —
Should he not hear them, — with the Turk.

Nay, start not from your chairs, in dread
   Of cannon-shot, or bursting shell !
These shall not fall upon your head,

As once upon your house they fell.
We have a weapon, firmer set,
And better than the bayonet; —

A weapon that comes down as still
    As snow-flakes fall upon the sod;
But executes a freeman's will
    As lightning does the will of God;
And from its force, nor doors nor locks
Can shield you; — 't is the ballot-box.

Black as your deed shall be the balls
    That from that box shall pour like hail!
And, when the storm upon you falls,
    How will your craven cheeks turn pale!
For, at its coming though ye laugh,
'T will sweep you from your hall, like chaff.

Not women, now, — the *people* pray.
    Hear us, — or *from* us ye will hear!
Beware! — a desperate game ye play!
    The men that thicken in your rear, —
Kings though ye be, — may not be scorned.
Look to your move! your stake! — YE 'RE WARNED.
    1837.

THE TOCSIN.

If the pulpit be silent, whenever or wherever there may be a sinner, bloody with this guilt, within the hearing of its voice, *the pulpit is false to its trust.*' — D. WEBSTER.

WAKE! children of the *men* who said,
  ' All are born free!' — Their spirits come
Back to the places where they bled
  In Freedom's holy martyrdom,
And find *you* sleeping on their graves,
And hugging there your chains, — ye slaves!

Ay, — slaves of slaves! What, sleep ye yet,
  And dream of Freedom, while ye sleep?
Ay, — dream, while Slavery's foot is set
  So firmly on your necks, — while deep
The chain, her quivering flesh endures,
Gnaws, like a cancer, into yours?

Hah! say ye that I 've falsely spoken,
　　Calling you slaves? — Then prove ye 're *not;*
Work a free press! — ye 'll see it broken; *
　　Stand to defend it! — ye 'll be shot. † —
O yes! but people should not dare
Print what 'the brotherhood' won't bear!

Then from your *lips* let words of grace,
　　Gleaned from the Holy Bible's pages,
Fall, while ye 're pleading for a race
　　Whose blood has flowed through chains for ages;
And pray, — 'Lord, let thy kingdom come!'
And *see* if ye 're not stricken dumb.

Yes, men of God! *ye* may not speak,
　　As, by the Word of God, ye 're bidden;
By the pressed lip, — the blanching cheek,
　　Ye feel yourselves rebuked and chidden; ‡

---

* Bear witness, heights of Alton!   † Bear witness, bones of Lovejoy!

‡ Bear witness, 'Grounds of Complaint preferred against the Rev. John
Pierpont, by a Committee of the Parish, called "The Proprietors of Hol-
lis-street Meetinghouse," to be submitted to an Ecclesiastical Council, as
Reasons for dissolving his Connexion with said Parish,' July 27th, 1840:
one of which runs thus; — Because 'of his too busy interference with
questions of legislation on the subject of prohibiting the sale of ardent
spirits; — of his too busy interference with questions of legislation on the

And, if ye 're not cast out, ye fear it; —
And why? — ' The brethren' will not hear it.

Since, then, through pulpit, or through press,
   To prove your freedom ye 're not able,
Go, — like the Sun of Righteousness,
   By wise men honored, — to a stable!
Bend *there* to Liberty your knee!
Say *there* that God made all men free!

Even there, — ere Freedom's vows ye 've plighted,
   Ere of her form ye 've caught a glimpse,
Even there are fires infernal lighted,
   And ye 're driven out by Slavery's imps. *

subject of imprisonment for debt; — of his too busy interference with the popular controversy on the subject of the abolition of slavery.' And this, in the eighteen hundred and fortieth year of Him whom the Lord sent ' to proclaim liberty to the captives, and the opening of the prison to them that are bound '!

  * Bear witness, that large ' upper room,' the hay-loft over the stable of the Marlborough Hotel, standing upon the ground now covered by the Marlborough Chapel; the only temple in Boston, into which the friends of human liberty, that is, of the liberty of man as *man*, irrespective of color or caste, could gain admittance for the annual meeting of the Massachusetts Anti-Slavery Society, January 25th, 1837 Bear witness, too, that smaller room in Summer street, where a meeting was held the same day, by members of the same Society; where their only altar was an iron stove, — their only incense, the fumes of a quantity of cayenne pepper, that some of the ' imps' had sprinkled upon the hot stove-plates, to drive the friends of the freedom of all men out of that little asylum.

Ah, well! — 'so persecuted they
The prophets' of a former day!

Go, then, and build yourselves a hall,
　　To prove ye are not slaves, but men!
Write 'FREEDOM,' on its towering wall!
　　Baptize it in the name of PENN;
And give it to her holy cause,
Beneath the Ægis of her laws; —

Within let Freedom's anthem swell; —
　　And, while your hearts begin to throb,
And burn within you —— Hark! the yell, —
　　The torch, — the torrent of the MOB! —
They 're Slavery's troops that round you sweep,
And leave your hall a smouldering heap! *

At Slavery's beck, the prayers ye urge
　　On your own servants, through the door
Of your own Senate, — that the scourge

* Bear witness, ye ruins of 'Pennsylvania Hall'! — a heap of ruins
made by a Philadelphia mob, May 17th, 1838, — and still allowed to re-
main a heap of ruins, as I was lately told in Philadelphia, from the fear,
on the part of the city government, that, should the noble structure be
reared again, and dedicated again to Liberty, the fiery tragedy of the 17th
of May would be *encored*.

May gash your brother's back no more, —
Are trampled underneath their feet,
While *ye* stand praying in the street!

At Slavery's beck, ye send your sons *
    To hunt down Indian wives or maids,
Doomed to the lash! — Yes, and their bones,
    Whitening 'mid swamps and everglades,
Where no friend goes to give them graves,
Prove that ye are not Slavery's slaves!

At Slavery's beck, the very hands
    Ye lift to Heaven, to swear ye 're free,
Will break a truce, to seize the lands
    Of Seminole or Cherokee!
Yes, — tear a *flag*, that Tartar hordes
Respect, and shield it with their swords! †

Vengeance is thine, Almighty God!
    To pay it hath thy justice bound thee;
Even now, I see thee take thy rod, —
    Thy thunders, leashed and growling round thee;

* Bear witness, Florida war, from first to last.
† Bear witness, ghost of the great-hearted, broken-hearted Osceola!

Slip them not yet, in mercy! — Deign
Thy wrath yet longer to restrain! —

Or, — let *thy* kingdom, Slavery, come!
　　Let Church, let State, receive thy chain!
Let pulpit, press, and hall be dumb,
　　If so 'the brotherhood' ordain!
The MUSE her own indignant spirit
Will yet speak out; — and men shall hear it.

Yes; — while, at Concord, there's a stone
　　That she can strike her fire from still;
While there's a shaft at Lexington,
　　Or half a one on Bunker's Hill, *
There shall she stand and strike her lyre,
And Truth and Freedom shall stand by her.

But, should she *thence* by mobs be driven,
　　For purer heights she'll plume her wing; —
Spurning a land of slaves, to heaven
　　She'll soar, where she can safely sing.
God of our fathers, speed her thither!
God of the free, let me go with her!
　　1838.

* The shaft on Bunker's Hill is now a whole one.

THE GAG.

———◆———

Ho ! children of the granite hills
   That bristle with the hackmatack,
And sparkle with the crystal rills
   That hurry toward the Merrimack,
Dam up those rills ! — for, while they run,
They all rebuke your Atherton.*

Dam up those rills ! — they flow so free
   O'er icy slope, o'er beetling crag,
That soon they 'll all be off at sea,
   Beyond the reach of Charlie's gag ; —
And when those waters are the sea's,
They 'll speak and thunder as they please !

---

   * I have no feelings of personal hostility towards the Hon. Charles G. Atherton. But if, by stifling the prayers of more than one million of his fellow men, in order that he may perpetuate the slavery of more than two millions, the best friend I have on earth shall seek to make his name immortal, I will do my best to — help him.

Then freeze them stiff! — but let there come
No *winds* to chain them; — should *they* blow,
They 'll speak of freedom; — let the dumb
And breathless frost forbid their flow.
Then, all will be so hushed and mum,
You 'll think your Atherton has come.

Not he! — ' Of all the airts * that blow,'
He dearly loves the soft South-west,
That tells where rice and cotton grow,
And man is, like the Patriarchs, blest
(So say some eloquent divines)
With God-given slaves † and concubines.

Let not the winds go thus at large,
That now o'er all your hills career, —
Your Sunapee and Kearsarge, —
Nay, nay, methinks the bounding deer
That, like the winds, sweep round their hill,
Should all be gagged, to keep them still.

* ' Of a' the airts the wind can blaw.' — *Burns.*

† ' Here we see God dealing in slaves,' &c. — *Sermon of the Rev. T. Clapp. New Orleans.*

And all your big and little brooks,
    That rush down laughing towards the sea,
Your Lampreys, Squams, and Contoocooks,
    That show a spirit to be free,
Should learn they 're not to take such airs; —
Your mouths are stopped; — then why not theirs?

Plug every spring that dares to play
    At bubble, in its gravel cup,
Or babble, as it runs away!
    Nay, — catch and coop your eagles up!
It is not meet that they should fly,
And scream of freedom, through your sky.

Ye 've not done yet! Your very trees, —
    Those sturdy pines, their heads that wag
In concert with the mountain breeze, —
    Unless they 're silenced by a gag,
Will whisper, — ' WE will stand our ground!
Our heads are *up!* OUR HEARTS ARE SOUND!

Yea, Atherton, the *upright* firs
    O er thee exult, and taunt thee thus, —
' Though THOU art fallen, no feller stirs

His foot, or lifts his axe at us.*
" Hell from beneath, is moved at thee,"
Since thou hast crouched to Slavery.

' Thou saidst, " I will exalt my throne
    Above the stars; and, in the north
Will sit upon the mount alone,
    And send my Slavery ' Orders' forth " !
Our WHITE HILLS spurn thee from their sight;
Their blasts shall speed thee in thy flight.

' Go! breathe amid the aguish damps
    That gather o'er the Congaree ; —
Go! hide thee in the cypress swamps
    That darken o'er the black Santee, —
And be the moss, above thy head,
The gloomy drapery of thy bed!

' The moss, that creeps from bough to bough,
    And hangs in many a dull festoon ; —

---

* ' Yea, the fir trees rejoice at thee, and the cedars of Lebanon, saying,
Since thou art laid down, no feller is come up against us. Hell, from be-
neath, is moved for thee, to meet thee at thy coming. — For thou hast said
in thy heart, I will ascend into heaven, I will exalt myself above the stars
of God ; I will sit also upon the mount of the congregation, in the sides
of the north.' — *Isaiah*, xiv. 8, 9, 13.

There, peeping through thy curtain, thou *
   Mayest catch some "glimpses of the moon";
Or, better, twist of it a string,
Noose in thy neck, repent, and — swing!'

Sons of the granite hills, your birds,
   Your winds, your waters, and your trees,
Of faith and freedom speak, in words
   That should be felt in times like these;
Their voice comes to you from the sky!
In them, GOD speaks of Liberty.

Sons of the granite hills, awake!
   Ye 're on a mighty stream afloat,
With all your liberties at stake; —
   A faithless pilot 's on your boat!
And, while ye 've lain asleep, ye 're snagged!
Nor can ye cry for help, — YE 'RE GAGGED!
   1839.

* These fir trees that grow upon the granite hills, though they seem to
have some *heart*, can certainly have no bowels, or only granite ones, else
they could never give such suicidal counsel.

3

THE CHAIN.

Is it his daily toil, that wrings
　　From the slave's bosom that deep sigh?
Is it his niggard fare, that brings
　　The tear into his down-cast eye?

O no; by toil and humble fare,
　　Earth's sons their health and vigor gain;
It is because he slave must wear
　　　　　　His chain.

Is it the sweat, from every pore
　　That starts, and glistens in the sun,
As, the young cotton bending o'er,
　　His naked back it shines upon?

Is it the drops that, from his breast,
   Into the thirsty furrow fall,
That scald his soul, deny him rest,
   And turn his cup of life to gall?

No; — for, that man with sweating brow
   Shall eat his bread, doth God ordain;
This the slave's spirit doth not bow;
            It is his chain.

Is it, that scorching sands and skies
   Upon his velvet skin have set
A hue, admired in beauty's eyes,
   In Genoa's silks, and polished jet?

No; for this color was his pride,
   When roaming o'er his native plain;
Even here, his hue can he abide,
           But not his chain.

Nor is it, that his back and limbs
   Are scored with many a gory gash,
That his heart bleeds, and his brain swims,
   And the MAN dies beneath the lash.

For Baäl's priests, on Carmel's slope,
　　Themselves with knives and lancets scored,
Till the blood spirted, — in the hope
　　The god would hear, whom they adored; —

And Christian flagellants their backs,
　　All naked, to the scourge have given;
And martyrs to their stakes and racks
　　Have gone, of choice, in hope of heaven; —

For here there was an inward WILL!
　　Here spake the spirit, upward tending;
And o'er Faith's cloud-girt altar, still,
　　Hope hung her rainbow, heavenward bending.

But will and hope hath not the slave,
　　His bleeding spirit to sustain: —
No, — he must drag on, to the grave,
　　　　　His chain.

　　1839.

THE FUGITIVE SLAVE'S APOSTROPHE TO THE NORTH STAR.

STAR of the North! though night-winds drift
   The fleecy drapery of the sky,
Between thy lamp and me, I lift,
   Yea, lift with hope, my sleepless eye,
To the blue heights wherein thou dwellest,
And of a land of freedom tellest.

Star of the North! while blazing day
   Pours round me its full tide of light,
And hides thy pale but faithful ray,
   I, too, lie hid, and long for night:
For night; — I dare not walk at noon,
Nor dare I trust the faithless moon, —

Nor faithless man, whose burning lust
　　For gold hath riveted my chain;
No other leader can I trust,
　　But thee, of even the starry train;
For, all the host around thee burning,
Like faithless man, keep turning, turning.

I may not follow where *they* go:
　　Star of the North, I look to thee,
While on I press; for well I know
　　Thy light and truth shall set me free; —
Thy light, that no poor slave deceiveth;
Thy truth, that all my soul believeth.

They of the East beheld the star
　　That over Bethlehem's manger glowed;
With joy they hailed it from afar,
　　And followed where it marked the road,
Till, where its rays directly fell,
They found the hope of Israel.

Wise were the men, who followed thus
　　The star that sets man free from sin!
Star of the North! thou art to us, —

Who 're slaves because we wear a skin
Dark as is night's protecting wing, —
Thou art to us a holy thing.

And we are wise to follow thee!
    I trust thy steady light alone:
Star of the North! thou seem'st to me
    To burn before the Almighty's throne,
To guide me, through these forests dim
And vast, to liberty and HIM.

Thy beam is on the glassy breast
    Of the still spring, upon whose brink
I lay my weary limbs to rest,
    And bow my parching lips to drink.
Guide of the friendless negro's way,
I bless thee for this quiet ray!

In the dark top of southern pines
    I nestled, when the driver's horn
Called to the field, in lengthening lines,
    My fellows, at the break of morn.
And there I lay, till thy sweet face
    Looked in upon 'my hiding-place.'

The tangled cane-brake, — where I crept,
  For shelter from the heat of noon,
And where, while others toiled, I slept,
  Till wakened by the rising moon, —
As its stalks felt the night-wind free,
Gave me to catch a glimpse of thee.

Star of the North! in bright array,
  The constellations round thee sweep,
Each holding on its nightly way,
  Rising, or sinking in the deep,
And, as it hangs in mid heaven flaming,
The homage of some nation claiming.

This nation to the Eagle * cowers;
  Fit ensign! she's a bird of spoil; —
Like worships like! for each devours
  The earnings of another's toil.
I've felt her talons and her beak,
And now the gentler Lion seek.

The Lion, at the Virgin's feet,
  Couches, and lays his mighty paw

---

* The constellations, *Aquila, Leo,* and *Virgo,* are here meant by the as-
tronomical fugitive.

Into her lap! — an emblem meet
　　Of England's Queen and English law : —
Queen, that hath made her Islands free!
Law that holds out its shield to me!

Star of the North! upon that shield
　　Thou shinest! — O, for ever shine!
The negro, from the cotton-field,
　　Shall then beneath its orb recline,
And feed the Lion couched before it,
Nor heed the Eagle screaming o'er it!
　　1839.

SLAVEHOLDER'S ADDRESS TO THE NORTH STAR.

STAR of the North, thou art not bigger
  Than is the diamond in my ring;
Yet every black, star-gazing nigger
  Stares at thee, as at some great thing!
Yes, gazes at thee, till the lazy
And thankless rascal is half crazy.

Some Quaker scoundrel must have told 'em
  That, if they take their flight tow'rd thee,
They 'd get where 'massa' cannot hold 'em;
  And, therefore, to the North they flee.
Fools! to be led off, where they can't earn
Their living, by thy lying lantern.

Thou 'rt a cold water star, I reckon,
　　Although I 've never seen thee, yet,
When to the bath thy sisters beckon,
　　Get even thy golden sandals wet;
Nor in the wave have known thee dip,
In our hot nights, thy finger's tip.

If thou *wouldst*, nightly, leave the pole,
　　To enjoy a regular ablution
In the North Sea, or Symmes's hole,
　　Our ' Patriarchal Institution,'
From which thou findest many a ransom,
Would, doubtless, give thee something handsome.

Although thou 'rt a cold water star,
　　As I have said, I think, already,
Thou 'rt hailed, by many a tipsy tar,
　　Who likes thee just because thou 'rt steady,
And hold'st the candle for the rover,
When he is more than ' half seas over.'

But, while Ham's seed, our land to bless,
　' Increase and multiply' like rabbits,
We like thee, Yankee Star, the less,

For thy bright eye, and steady habits.
Pray waltz with Venus, star of love,
Or take a bout with reeling Jove.

Thou art an abolition star,
    And to my wench wilt be of use, if her
Dark eye should find thee, ere the car
    Of our true old slave-catcher, ' Lucifer,
Star of the morning,' upward rolls,
And, with its light, puts out the pole's.

On our field hands thou lookest, too —
    A sort of nightly overseer —
Canst find no other work to do?
    I tell thee, thou 'rt not wanted here ;
So, pray, shine only on the oceans,
Thou number one of ' Northern notions.'

Yes, northern notions, — northern lights !
    As hates the devil holy water,
So hate I all that Rogers writes,
    Or Weld, that married Grimkè's daughter : —
So hate I all these northern curses,
From Birney's prose to Whittier's verses.

' Put out the light!' exclaimed the Moor —
   I think they call his name Othello —
When opening his wife's chamber door
   To cut her throat — the princely fellow!
Noblest of all the nigger nation!
File leader in amalgamation!

' Put out the light!' and so say I.
   Could ' I quench *thee*, thou flaming minister,'
No longer, in the northern sky,
   Should blaze thy beacon-fire so sinister.
North Star, thy light's unwelcome — *very* —
We 'll vote thee ' an incendiary.'

And, to our ' natural allies ' —
   Our veteran Kinderhook Invincibles,
Who do our bidding, in the guise
   Of ' northern men, with southern principles,'—
Men who have faces firm as dough,
And, as we *set* their noses, go —

To these, we 'll get some scribe to write,
   And tell them not to let thee shine —
Excepting of a cloudy night —

Any where, south of Dixon's line.
If, beyond that, thou shin'st, an inch,
We 'll have thee up before Judge Lynch : —

And when, thou abolition star,
    Who preachest freedom, in all weathers,
Thou hast got on a coat of tar,
    And, over that, a cloak of feathers,
That thou art 'fixed' shall none deny,
If there 's a fixed star in the sky.

ECONOMY OF SLAVERY.

———◆———

' ONE mouth and one back to two hands,' is the law,
　That the hand of his Maker has stamped upon
　　man;
But Slavery lays on God's image her paw,
　And fixes him out on a different plan; —
Two mouths and *two* backs to two hands she cre-
　　ates;
　And the consequence is, as she might have ex-
　　pected;
Let the hands do their best, upon all her estates,
　The mouths go half fed, and the backs half pro-
　　tected.
　　1840.

PLYMOUTH ROCK.

ESCAPED from all the perils of the sea, —
   Storms, shoals, — the angry and engulphing
      waves, —
Here stand we, on a savage shore, — all free,
   Thy freemen, Lord! and not of man the slaves.
   Here will we toil and serve thee, till our graves
On these bleak hills shall open. — When the blood
   Thou pourest now so warm along our veins
Shall westward flow, till Mississippi's flood
   Gives to our children's children his broad plains,
   Ne'er let them *wear*, O God, or *forge* a bondman's
      chains!

    1840.

THE LIBERTY BELL.

The Liberty Bell — the Liberty Bell —
The Tocsin of Freedom and Slavery's knell,
That a whole long year has idle hung,
Again is wagging its clamorous tongue !
    As it merrily swings,
    Its notes it flings

4

On the dreamy ears of planters and kings;
 And it gives them a token
 Of manacles broken;
And all that the prophets of Freedom have spoken,
 With tongues of flame,
 Like those which came
On the men who first spoke in the Saviour's name,
 Comes over their soul,
 As death-bells knoll,
Or the wheels of coming thunder roll!
 Our Liberty Bell —
 They know it well,
The Tocsin of Freedom and Slavery's knell!

Our Liberty Bell! let its startling tone
Abroad o'er a slavish land be thrown!
Nay, on the wings of the north-east wind,
Let it reach the isles of the Western Ind —
 Those isles of the sun,
 Where the work is done,
That, here at the North, is but just begun.
 Let the Bell be swung,
 Till old and young,

That dwell New-England's hills among,
    Shall wake at the peal,
    And, with holy zeal,
Beside their mountain altars kneel,
    And pray that the yoke
    From the necks may be broke
Of the millions who feel the 'continual stroke'
    Of the despot's rod;
    And that earth's green sod
No more by the foot of a slave may be trod.

Let the Liberty Bell ring out — ring out!
And let freemen reply, with a thundering shout,
That the gory scourges and clanking chains,
That blast the beauty of Southern plains,
    Shall be stamped in the dust;
    And that thrice-gorged Lust,
That gloats on his helpless bond-maid's bust,
    Ere long shall see
    That slave set free,
And joining in Liberty's Jubilee.
    That Jubilee song!
    ' O Lord, how long'

Must the world yet wait for that Jubilee song?
  Yet, come it must;
  Jehovah is just,
And his Truth and his Spirit we cheerfully trust.
  That Truth to tell,
  Comes the Liberty Bell,
And that Spirit shall make it strike Slavery's knell.

Our Liberty Bell! let its solemn chime
Fall on the ear of hoary Time,
As onward — onward to its goal,
He sees the chariot of Liberty roll;
  While with shout and song,
  The swelling throng
Of the friends of the bondman urge it along.
  Let the same chime fall
  On the ears of all,
Who tread on the neck of the negro thrall,
  Till they start from the ground,
  As they will at the sound,
When the trumpets of angels are pealing around,
  And the murdered slave
  Comes forth from his grave,

And smiles at the flash of th' Avenger's glaive;
   And the world shall accord
   In the righteous award
To both tyrant and slave, in that day of the Lord!

  1842.

TO ABOLITIONISTS.

SERVANTS of God most high,
　Who on his word rely,
By ancient seers and holy prophets spoken —
　That all the chains that gall
　The Ethiopian thrall,
And every yoke, shall from his neck be broken —

　Whether, with holy zeal,
　Ye in your closets kneel,
Or plead the cause of Freedom in a throng,
　Or through a dauntless press,
　The voice of righteousness
Ye pour out, like a torrent, deep and strong —

Give not your labors o'er,
Because ye 're few and poor,
Because a lion couches in your path,
Because a lawless horde
Upon your heads have poured, —
Your heads unhelmeted, — their vialed wrath.

The ancient seers, like you,
To God and duty true,
Were, in their day, reviled and put to shame :
Scorned, hated, hunted, they
From earth have passed away :
Their forms have passed away, but not their fame.

Death dares not touch their *Word!*
The soul of man is stirred
By it, wherever on the darkling earth,
God's Truth and human Right
Come down to dwell in light,
And holy Freedom struggles into birth.

So shall *your* words be breathed,
Where'er man's brow is wreathed
With the sharp chaplet that for Him was twined,

Who lived mid taunts and sneers,
Who died mid scoffs and jeers,
From sin and slavery to redeem mankind.

Servants of God most holy,
Who stoop to man most lowly,
To lift him up and give him liberty,
What though to-day's unpleasant!
Ye live not in the present;
Your life is in the infinite TO BE.

Your words of love sincere,
Now spoken in the ear,
Where Mammon's priests bend at his altar brazen,
And lift the suppliant eye,
In foul idolatry —
All tongues shall trumpet, and on house-tops blazon.

Yea, and your 'name and praise,'
That, in these slavish days,
So many vainly dream are soon to perish,
As in the coming age
They shine on History's page,
The proud shall envy, and the good shall cherish.
1842.

DEATH OF CHARLES FOLLEN.

———◆———

Written for the Funeral Service in Commemoration of the Life and
Character of CHARLES FOLLEN, before the Massachusetts Anti-Slavery
Society, April 17th, 1840. Address by Samuel J. May.

———

O, NOT for thee weep; — we weep
  For her, whose lone and long caress,
And widow's tears, from fountains deep,
  Fall on the early fatherless.

'T is for ourselves we mourn; — we mourn
  Our blighted hopes, our wishes crossed,
Thy strength, that hath our burdens borne,
  Thy love, thy smile, thy counsels lost.

'T is for the slave we sigh : — we sigh
    To think thou sleepest on a shore
Where thy calm voice and beaming eye
    Shall plead the bondman's cause no more.

'T is for our land we grieve : — we grieve
    That Freedom's fane, Devotion's shrine,
And Faith's fresh altar, thou should'st leave,
    And they all lose a soul like thine.

A soul like thine — so true a soul,
    Wife, friends, our land, the world must miss :
The waters o'er thy corse may roll,
    But thy pure spirit is in bliss.

HYMN FOR THE FIRST OF AUGUST.

————◆————

WHERE Britannia's emerald isles
　　Gem the Caribbean sea,
And an endless summer smiles,
　　Lo! the negro thrall is free!
Yet not on Columbia's plains,
　　Hath the sun of freedom risen:
Here, in darkness and in chains,
　　Toiling millions pine in prison.

Shout! ye islands disenthralled,
　　Point the finger, as in scorn,
At a country that is called
　　Freedom's home, where men are born

Heirs, for life, to chains and whips, —
  Bondmen, who have never known
Wife, child, parent, that their lips
  Ever dared to call their own.

Yet, a *Christian* land is this!
  Yea, and ministers of Christ
Slavery's foot, in homage, kiss;
  And their brother, who is priced
Higher than their Saviour, even,
  Do they into bondage sell; —
Pleading thus the cause of Heaven,
  Serving thus the cause of hell.

Holy Father, let thy word,
  Spoken by thy prophets old,
By the pliant priest be heard;
  And let lips, that now are cold,
(Chilled by Mammon's golden wand!)
  With our nation's 'burden' glow,
Till the free man and the bond
  Shout for Slavery's overthrow!

1842.

PRAYER OF THE ABOLITIONIST.

WE ask not that the slave should lie,
  As lies his master, at his ease,
Beneath a silken canopy,
  Or in the shade of blooming trees.

We mourn not that the man should toil;
  'T is nature's need — 't is God's decree;
But, let the hand that tills the soil,
  Be, like the wind that fans it, free.

We ask not 'eye for eye' — that all,
  Who forge the chain and ply the whip,
Should feel their torture — that the thrall
  Should wield the scourge of mastership —

We only ask, O God, that they,
  Who bind a brother, may relent:
But, GREAT AVENGER, we do pray
  That the wrong-doer may repent.
1842.

UNCHAIN THE LABORER.

STRIKE from that laborer's limbs his chain!
  In the fierce sun the iron burns!
By night, it fills his dreams with pain;
  By day, it galls him as he turns.

Yes; and *your* dreams it visits, too,
  When Fear stands o'er your restless bed,
And shakes it in your ears, till you
  Tremble, as at an earthquake's tread.

Then break his chain, and let him go,
  And, with the spirit of a man,
Earn his own bread; and you shall know
  Peace, — that you know not now, nor can

The chain, that binds to you your slave,
  Binds you to him, with links so strong,
That you must wear them to your grave,
  If all your days you do him wrong.

Then, from his body and your soul,
  Throw off the load, while yet you may;
Thus strive, in faith, for heaven's high goal,
  And wait, in hope, the judgement day.
1842.

PRAYER FOR THE SLAVE.

———◆———

Almighty God ! thou Giver
  Of all our sunny plains,
That stretch from sea to river,
  Hear'st thou thy children's chains?
Seest thou the snappered lashes,
  That daily sting, afresh?
Seest thou the cow-skin's gashes,
  Cut through the quivering flesh?

Seest thou the sores, that rankle,
  Licked by no pitying dog,
Where, round the bondman's ancle,
  They 've rivetted a clog?

5

Hear'st thou the curse he mutters?
   Seest thou his flashing eye?
Hear'st thou the prayer he utters,
   That thou would'st let him die?

God of the poor and friendless,
   Shall this unequalled wrong,
This agony, be endless?
   How long, O Lord, how long
Shall man set, on his brother,
   The iron heel of sin,
The Holy Ghost to smother —
   To crush the God within!

Call out, O God, thy legions —
   The hosts of love and light!
Ev'n in the blasted regions
   That Slavery wraps in night,
Some of thine own anointed
   Shall catch the welcome call,
And, at the hour appointed,
   Do battle for the thrall.

Let press, let pulpit thunder,
   In all slaveholders' ears,
Till they disgorge the plunder,
   They 've garnered up, for years;
Till Mississippi's Valley,
   Till Carolina's coast,
Round Freedom's standard rally,
   A vast, a *ransomed* host!
1842.

ODE,

Sung by the Constituents of JOHN QUINCY ADAMS, on his return from
Congress, September 17, 1842.

———◆———

NOT from the bloody field,
Borne on his battered shield,
    By foes o'ercome,
But, from a sterner fight,
In the defence of Right,
Clothed in a conquerer's might,
    We hail him home.

Where Slavery's minions cower
Before the servile power,
    He bore their ban;
And, like an aged oak,
That braved the lightning's stroke,
When thunders round it broke,
    Stood up, A MAN.

Nay — when they stormed aloud,
And round him, like a cloud,
    Came, thick and black,
He, single-handed, strove,
And, like Olympian Jove,
With his own thunder, drove
    The phalanx back.

No leafy wreath we twine,
Of oak or Isthmian pine,
    To grace his brow;
Like his own locks of gray,
Such leaves would fall away,
As will the grateful lay,
    We weave him now.

But Time shall touch the page,
That tells how Quincy's sage
    Has dared to live,
Save as he touches wine,
Or Shakspeare's glowing line,
Or Raphael's forms divine,
    New life to give.

'I WOULD NOT LIVE ALWAYS.'

I WOULD not live always; I ask not to stay,
Where I *must* bear the burden and heat of the day :
Where my body is cut with the lash or the cord,
And a hovel and hunger are all my reward.

I would not live always, where life is a load
To the flesh and the spirit : — since there's an abode
For the soul disenthralled, let me breathe my last
          breath,
And repose in thine arms, my deliverer, Death ! —

I would not live always to toil as a slave :
O no, let me rest, though I rest in my grave ;
For there, from their troubling, the wicked shall
          cease,
And, free from his master, the slave be at peace.
    1843.

OFT, IN THE CHILLY NIGHT.

OFT, in the chilly night,
  Ere slumber's chain has bound me,
When all her silvery light
  The moon is pouring round me,
      Beneath her ray,
      I kneel and pray,
  That God would give some token,
      That Slavery's chains,
      On southern plains,
  Shall all, ere long, be broken.
Yes, in the chilly night,
  Though Slavery's chain has bound me,
Kneel I, and feel the might
  Of God's right arm around me.

When, at the driver's call,
  In cold or sultry weather,
We slaves, both great and small,
  Turn out to toil together,
      I feel like one,
      From whom the sun
Of hope has long departed,
      And morning's light,
      And weary night
Still find me broken-hearted.
Thus when the chilly breath
  Of night is sighing round me,
Kneel I, and wish that Death,
  In his cold chain, had bound me.
1843.